Merâas

LEGACY

A collection of Inspirational Poetry

SHAGUFTA QURESHI

MERÂAS
LEGACY

iUniverse books may be ordered through booksellers or by contacting:

iUniverse
1663 Liberty Drive
Bloomington, IN 47403
www.iuniverse.com
1-800-Authors (1-800-288-4677)

ISBN: 978-1-5320-6714-3 (sc)
ISBN: 978-1-5320-6713-6 (e)

Library of Congress Control Number: 2019900938

Print information available on the last page.

iUniverse rev. date: 02/20/2019

Dedication

I want to dedicate my book to my mother Salma Sultana, who also wrote poetry and inspired me to voice my thoughts through poetry.

Special Thanks

I would like to thank my husband Yahya Qureshi, my daughter Maheen Qureshi and my son Haseeb Qureshi for helping me with the translation.

I also would like to thank Yahya Qureshi for providing the photographed cover of my book.

Without all of your help and support, this wouldn't be possible.

Key to transcription of Urdu into Roman

1. Vowels

Examples			
1: Short	**Long**	**Short**	**Long**
a	â	ab	âj
i	ï	in	bïn
o	ô	ko	bôl
u	ü	sun	süna
e	ê	ke	dêkh
ai	aï	la	baïn

2. Nasal sounds

Examples - These are indicated by the sign ~ above the n following the vowel

Non nasalized	Nasalized	Non nasalized	Nasalized
â	âñ	mân	mâñ
ï	iñ	bin	nahiñ
u	uñ	un	kyüñ

3. Consonants particular to Urdu

kh	خ	khâs
q	ق	qarïb
a'	ع	a' dl
gh	غ	ghalib
ch	چ	châñd

Contents

وہ کچھ اَن سُنی سی باتیں
وہ کچھ اَن کہی سی یادیں

جو زبن کی کسی کہانی میں
کہیں دُور یوں ہیں پڑی ہوئی

جیسے کوئی بوسیدہ کتاب
کہیں گرد میں ہے اٹی ہوئی

چلو آج پھر چلیں ہم
کوئی ورق اور تھلیں ہم

کسی یاد کا پُرانا
کوئی موڑ ہو سُہانا

جہاں چند گھڑی بھٹک کر
تھوڑا اور جی اُٹھیں ہم

وہ کچھ اَن سُنی سی باتیں
وہ کچھ اَن کہی سی یادیں

چلو آؤ پھر چلیں ہم
کہیں دور یادوں کے دیس میں

کہیں اپنا بچپن تلاش لیں
کوئی بیتے لمحے اُدھار لیں

وہ کہیں جو اب تک کہا نہیں
وہ سُنیں جو کب سے سُنا نہیں

چلو آؤ دُھول کو جھاڑ کر
کوئی میٹھی یاد پھر نکال لیں

چلو آج پھر سے یہ جان لیں
ایک شام اور سنوار لیں

اس زندگی کی کتاب کو
چلو ورقہ ورقہ گزار لیں

شگفتہ قریشی
مئی 14، 2012

Yâadaiñ (1)

Vô kuch un-sunï sï bâataiñ
Vô kuch un-kahï sï yâadaiñ

Jo zahen kï kissï khâï meiñ
Kahïñ dôor yôñ hai parï hovï

Jaysay kôï bôosêdâ kitâab
Kahïñ gûrd meiñ hai attï hovï

Chalo âaj phïr chalaiñ hum
Koï warq aur thalaiñ hum

Kisï yâad kâ purânâ
Koï mor hô suhâanâ

Jahañ chund ghrêe bhatak kar
Thorâ aur jêe uthaiñ hum

Vô kuch un-kahï sï bâataiñ
Vô kuch un-sunï sï yâadaiñ

Chalo âao phïr chalaiñ hum
Kahiñ door yâadôñ ke dais maiñ

Kahiñ apnâ bachpan talâash-leñ
Koi bêete lamhe udhâr leñ

Vô kahaiñ Jo ab-tak kahâ nahï
Vô sou-naiñ Jo kab se sunâ nahï

Chalo âao dhôol ko jahâar kar
Koï methï yâad phïr nikâal leñ

Chalo âaj phïr se ye jâan leñ
Aik shâam aur sanwâr leñ

Es zindagï kï kitâab kô
Challo warqâ warqâ guzar leñ.

Memories (1)

Those few unheard conversations.
Those few unsaid memories.

Hidden deep in the crevice of our minds,
Like an old, forgotten book, somewhere under the dirt.

Let us today, open another page, and find a pleasant junction of old memories.

Where we can wonder and relive those old memories, just for a while.

Let's look for our childhood again.
Let's borrow some precious moments from our past.

Let's say what we have not spoken yet.
Let's hear what we have not heard yet.

Let's wipe the dirt off.
Let's find another sweet memory.

Let's learn it together.
Let's make another evening beautiful.

Let's go over the book of life, one page at a time.

Those few unheard conversations.
Those few unsaid memories

May 14, 2012

دُور کہیں میرا آشیانہ تھا
آشیانے میں ایک گھرانہ تھا
ماں تھی بابا تھے اور تھے لوگ ہزار
پیار کرنے والے سب رشتہ دار

آشیانے کے دن سُہانے تھے
اُس کی راتوں میں تھے ہزاروں چراغ
چھوٹی چھوٹی سی ننھی کلیاں تھیں
بابا کے نازوں میں وہ پلیاں تھیں

دھیرے دھیرے سے اُن کو سینچا تھا
گھر میں بس چاندنی کا ڈیرہ تھا
ننھی کلیاں جو اب جوان ہوئیں
گھر کی گلیاں جیسے ویران ہوئیں

اُن کو اب اور نگر جانا تھا
دیس اپنا کوئی بسانا تھا
تھا فکر کیسے بھول پائیں گے
یہ جو گلیاں وہ چھوڑ جائیں گے

کرنی کوئی خدا نے ایسی کی
گھر میں راحت خدا نے ایسی دی
بھول کر اپنے آشیانے کو
راحتیں دے دیں اس گھرانے کو

اب یہاں چاندنی کا ڈیرہ ہے
روشنی کا کوئی بسیرہ ہے
زندگی اپنے آب و تاب پہ ہے
چاند سورج بھی اُس شباب پہ ہے

گھر میں پھر ننھی ننھی کلیاں ہیں
بابا کے نازوں میں وہ پلیاں ہیں
ماں ہے بابا ہیں اور ہیں لوگ ہزار
پیار کرنے والے سب رشتہ دار

لوگ ہر دور آئیں جائیں گے
آشیانے کئی بنائیں گے
بات اتنی صرف سمجھ لو تم
پیار بانٹو، تو پیار پا لو تم

زندگی چیز آنی جانی ہے
بیت جائے جو، وہ کہانی ہے
بھر دو تم اسکو اپنے رنگوں سے
پھر بنے امر جو کہانی ہے

سوچتی تھی کہانی ختم ہوئی
زندگی یہ سُہانی ختم ہوئی
یہ تو قدرت کا ایک کرشمہ ہے
زندگی کو تو یوں ہی چلنا ہے

شگفتہ قریشی
2/10/2012

Marï kahânï (2)

Dôor kahiñ merâ âshïyânâ thâ
Âshïyâne meiñ aik gharânâ thâ
Mâa thï babâ thay aur thay log hazâr
Pyâr karne wale sab rïshte-dâr

Âshïyâne ke dïn suhâne thay
Us kï râtoñ meiñ thay hazâroñ chirâgh
Chotï chotï sï nanhï kalyañ theen
Baba ke nazon se vo puliyan thêeñ

Dhêere dhêere se un ko sañchâ thâ
Ghâr meiñ bus chandnï kâ dêerâ thâ
Nanhï kalïyañ Jo Ab jawân ho-eïñ
Ghar ki galiyâñ jesse veran ho-eiñ

Un ko ub aur nager Janâ thâ
Dais upnâ koï bassânâ thâ
Thâ fiker kaise bhôl pâyeñge
Ye Jo galiyâñ vo chôr jayeñge

Karnï koï khudâ ne essï kï
Ghar meiñ râhet khudâ ne essï dï
Bhôol kar apne âshïyâne ko
Râhteiñ de dï es gharâne ko

Ab yahâñ chandnï kâ derâ hai
Roshnï kâ koï besserâ hai
Zindagï apne âab-o-tâab pe hai
Chând süraj bhï us shabâb pe hai

Ghar meiñ phïr nanhï nanhï kalïyañ haiñ
Babâ ke nâzoñ meiñ vo palïyañ haiñ
Mâa hai babâ hai aur hai log hazâr
Pyâr karne wale sab rishtâ-dâr

log her dur âyaiñ jâyaiñ-gy
Âshïyâne kaï benâiñ gy
Bâat itnï sarf samjh lo tum
Pyâr banto tu pyâr pâa lo tum!

Zindagï chêez âni-jâni hai
Bêet jâye jo vo kahânï hai
Bhar du es ko tum apne rangoñ se
Sub kahiñ amar zindaganï hai

Sochtï thï kahanï khatum huï
Zindagï ye suhânï khatum huï
Ye tu qudrat kâ aik karïshmâ hai
Zindagï ko toh yoñhï chalnâ hai!

My story (2)

Somewhere far away was my home.
In my home belonged a family.
Maa was there, Baba was there, as were hundreds
of others.
Of loving nature, were these relatives.

In the days of dwelling, life was beautiful.
Its nights were illuminated by candles,
Little flower buds were blooming.
By Baba's care, these flower buds grew.

Slowly but surely, the children matured.
And the house was enlightened by pure moonlight.
The mischievous girls sprouted into beautiful women.
They left those intricate pathways and ponds.
Hence; the house grew empty.

The time came for the Children to migrate,
In search of their own life.
Worries weighed them.
How can they leave behind childhood memories?

However, the plans of God proceeded,
In their house he provides blessings.
He helped them find happiness in their new dwellings,
As they drifted from their old lives.

Moonlight enlightened the house once again.
Life is reaching its peak.
Life is now as it was, as vibrant as the sun and moon.

In the house, once again, little buds started to grow.
These little girls were loved and spoiled.
Maa was there, Baba was there, as were hundreds of others,
Of loving, nature were these relatives.

People will come and go.
Many roofs will be built in one's lifetime.
The important thing to understand is...
That you can only find love if you give love.

To live is to twist and turn without rhythm.
Life is a story with a limit.
To immortalize your story,
You must fill your life with the vibrant colors of love.

I used to think my story had ended,
That my beautiful life had reached its climax.
However, the charisma of nature is that life always goes on.
That's the circle of life.

February 12, 2012

زندگی کو پا لیا بچپن لُٹا دینے کے بعد
جان پائی یہ مگر قیمت چُکا دینے کے بعد

زندگی کی دوڑ میں سر مست ہم چلتے رہے
راستے گھٹتے رہے اور منزلیں بڑھتی رہیں

ایک مایہ جال بن کر رہ گئی ساری حیات
کچھ سُنانے کو نہیں اب بتاؤں دِل کی بات

دو گھڑی جو سوچنے کے واسطے بیٹھی اگر
ہر کسی کی زندگی میں بے کلی آئی نظر

کیا بتاؤں کیا ہے جانا عمر بتا دینے کے بعد
کھو دی جینے کی حقیقت منزلیں پانے کے بعد

ہر نفس اک لا حاصل دوڑ میں آیا نظر
موہ، مایہ حوس میں اب مبتلا ہے ہر بشر

کیا کہوں کہ کیا بچا کیا چھِن گیا اس دوڑ میں
منزلوں کو پا لیا مقصد گنوا دینے کے بعد !!!

شگفتہ قریشی

Farabe-e-Hayât. (3)

Zindagï ko pâ liyâ bachpan lotâ danè ke bâad
Jan pâaï ye magar qimat chukâ deney ke bâad

Zindagï kï dôr meiñ sar-mast hum chalte rahey
Raastey ghatay rahe aur manzelaiñ barhtï rahiñ

Aik mayajâal bun- ker reh gayï sâari hayâat
Kuch sunaney ko nahi ab kya bataaoñ dil kï bâat

Dū ghari jo sôchne ke vâste bethï agar
Her kisï ki zindegi meiñ bay-kalï âaï nazer

Kya bataaoñ kya hai jana omer betâ deney ke bâad
Kho di jeene ki haqeeqat manzileiñ paane ke bâad

Har nafas aik la hâasïl dôr meiñ âayâ nazar
Moh, maya hivas meiñ ab mubtala hai har bashar

Kya kahooñ ke kya bacha kya chein giya es dor meiñ
Manzelooñ ko pa leya maqsad genwa deney ke
bâad !

Delusion of Life (3)

We find life by sacrificing childhood,
However, we find out after paying the price.

In the race of life, we kept running frantically.
Distances kept getting shorter, but goals kept getting farther.

Life became a web of substance and materialism.
What can I tell you? There is nothing to say.

For a moment, I paused and thought about it,
I saw the same anguish in everyone's life.

What can I say, about what I learned, after spending my life?
After achieving the set goals, I had lost the meaning of life.
I realized that, as a race, we lost the purpose of life, despite achieving our goals.

Everyone seems to be running a meaningless race.
Humans are engulfed by greed, gluttony, and lust.

It is hard to access the gains and losses of life.
After achieving the set goals, I had lost the purpose of life.

Shagufta Qureshi
2/17/2018

ایک آدم اور حوا سے بنایا رَب نے
خاک سے جسم یہ خاکی بھی بنایا رَب نے

سوچا جب خاک سے پیوند کروں گا اسکو
دل میں کچھ اچھے بُرے اِلہام بھی دوں گا اِسکو

جا کے دنیا میں وہ میرا سبق دُھرائے گا
زندگی کیا ہے وہ سبکو یہ سکھلائے گا

پھینک دوں گا اِسے پھر جلتی ہوی دنیا میں
دیکھوں کیا رنگ جو بدلے گی یہ دنیا اسکے

ایک شطرنج کے مہُرے سے تو زیادہ تو نہیں
تیری اوقات ہے کیا تو میرا نائب تو نہیں

زیست کی آگ کہ آگے تو تو پروانہ ہے
تیرا اور کام ہے کیا جلتے چلے جانا ہے

پر اس آدم نے جو دنیا پہ قہر ڈھایا ہے
رب نے بھی توبہ کری خُدائی نے منہ چھپایا ہے

بھول کر خاک سے رشتے کو وہ جا ملا شیطان
مار کر اپنے ہی لوگوں کو بن گیا فرعون

بن گیا قاتلِ انسان تیرا بیٹا حوا
بن گیا رَب جسے بنایا تھا صرف انساں حوا

اُس کی ظلمت کی کہانی تو بڑی لمبی ہے
شکلیں بدلی ہیں لیکن بات بڑی لمبی ہے

کیسے جی پائیں ننگے اِس دنیا میں ڈر لگتا ہے
کیسے بچ پائیں گے ناسور سے ڈر لگتا ہے

خاک سے خاکی یہ بندہ بڑا شاطر نکلا

تھا بنایا جسے رب نے نائب صرف شیطاں نکلا

شگفتہ قریشی

مارچ 15, 2014

(4) Khâkï

Aik âadam aur howâ se banâyâ rûb ne.
Khâk se jïsm ye khâkï bhi banâyâ rub ne.

Sôchâ jab khâk se pevand kroñ gâ es ko.
Dïl meiñ khch achey burey elhâm bhï dôñ gâ es-ko.

Jâ-ke dunïyâ meiñ vo merâ sabak dohrâye gâ.
Zandagï keyâ hai vo sab ko ye sekhlâye gâ.

Phaink doñ gâ ïssay phïr Jaltï huï dunïyâ meiñ.
Dekho kiya rang Jo badlay-gï ye dunïyâ us kay.

Aik shtranj ke mohray se, tu zaidhâ tu nahï.
Tarï ôqâat hai kyâ tu merâ niyeb tu nahï.

Zêest kï âag ke âagay, tu tô per-wânâ hai.
Terâ aur kâm hai keyâ Jalte-chale Jânâ hai.

Per es âadum ne, Jo duniyâ pe qaher dhâyâ hai.
Rub ne bhï tobâ Karï, khudâaï ne-muh chpâyâ hai.

Bhôol ker khâk se rishtay ko, vo Jâ milâ shetâan.
Mâr ke apne hï lôgôñ kô, bun-geyâ fïrôñ.

Bun-geyâ qâtil-e-insâañ terâ betâ huwâ.
Bun-geyâ rub, jessay banâyâ thâ siruf insâañ hawâ.

Us ki zulmât kï kahânï, tu barï lambï hai.
Shakleiñ badlï heiñ, Lekïn bâat Barï lambï hai.

Kessy jï pâyaiñ-gay es duniyâ meiñ, dar lagtâ hai.
Kessy buch Payiñ gay nâsôor se, dar lagtâ hai.

Khâk se khâkï ye Bandâ, berâ shâater nïklâ
Thâ benâyâ jissay rab ne nâyib, sarif shetâan niklâ.

(4) Clay to Skin

I created humankind from Adam and Eve,
Using dirt, I morphed their bodies.

I decided when I formed the skin with dirt,
To give man, both good and evil will.

You will echo my message in the world.
You will tell them the meaning of life.

I put you in that burning world,
Also, saw how it molded you, for you...

You are not more than a chess piece.
You are nobody, not a subordinate of mine.
You are like a moth to the flame of life.
Your destiny is to burn and keep burning.

However, man created chaos in this world.
I, the creator, am hiding my face, ashamed of
humankind's misdeed

The man has forgotten his relations with the dirt and
has become a companion of evil.
By killing his people, he turned into non-other than
a Pharaoh.

Your son has become a murderer, Eve.
He became a god when he was supposed to only
be human.

The story of man's darkness is inevitable.
Its history wears many masks of ever-changing
faces, but its story remains the same.

How can anyone survive in this world, I fear?
How can humankind be safe from this cancer, I fear?

This man that I created with the dirt turned out to be cunning.
One who was created as an envoy of God turned out to be the subject of Evil.

March 15, 2014

جد سال ہا سال دے ورتن توں
اے پیار دی چادر چھِج جاوے

جد روز حیاتی گزرن توں
کجھ دلاں دی دوری ودھ جاوے

جد رشتیاں دے تقدس دا
سب تانا بانا کھلر جاوے

تد صبر دا دھاگہ لبھ لئے
تے پیار دی سوی بنڑ جیائے

فیر کھجی ہوئی ایس چادر دا
کوئی اک کنارا پھڑ لئے

فیر ہولے ہولے پیار دے نال
سب تانا بانا گنڈھ لئے

نہ ویکھئے کی میلدا اے
نہ سوچئے کون ویندا اے

ایس میلی کھجی چادر نوں
فیر ہولئے ہولئے پنڑ لئے

ایہہ پیار تے کوئی دیوا اے
جیہڑا میٹھی اگ سلگدا اے

اوہ کسے فقیر دی جھگی وچ
کینی لاٹاں نالوں بلدا اے

اے شئے بڑی انمول اے
توں سدا ایس دا دھیان رکھیں

کدی بھل کہ وی ایہ سوچیں نہ
کہ مینوں ایتھوں کی میلدا اے

ایہ جنت دا کوئی میوہ اے
جیھڑا مٹھیاں توں وی مٹھا اے

جو پیار تے صبر دے ورتن توں
بس ہولے ہولے پھلدا اے۔

شگفتہ قریشی
6/22/2015

(5) Pyâr dï Châder

Judh sâl-hâ-sâl de verton toñ
Aye pyâr dï châder chejh jâve

Judh rôz hayâtï guzrun toñ
Kujh dilâñ dï doorï wadh jâve

Judh reshteyâñ dae taqadus dâ
Sub tanâ-banâ khelûr jâve

Tudh saber dâ tâagâ lubh laiye
Te pyâr dï suï bañ jâye

Phir kejhï hôï es châder dâ
Koï aik kenârâ phûr laïye

Phïr holay holay pyâr de nâl
Sub tânâ-bânâ gundh laiye

Nâ wakhïye kï mildâ ae
Nâ sochïye kon wayndâ ae

Aes maylï khejï châder nü
Phïr holay holay pünh laïye

Ae pyâr teh koï dëwâ ae
Jehrâ mithï aüg sulagdhâ ae

Öo kisï fakêr dï chugï wïch
Kinï lâtâañ nâloñ buldâ ae

Ae shay barï unmôl ae
Toñ sadâ aiss dâ teyân rakhêeñ

Kade bhül key vï ea sôcheïñ nâ
Kay meno aythôñ kï mildâ ae

Ae janat dâ koï meevâ ae
Jerâ methayâañ toñ vï methâ ae

Jô pyâr tey saber de vartoñ toñ
Bus holay holay Phuldâ ae !

(5) Drape of love

The drape of love gets damaged, by continually using it over the years.

Hearts begin to drift apart, as one's daily life continues.

When the respect in a relationship becomes disfigured,
Find the thread of patience and become a needle of love to sew it back.

Then grab ahold of one end of the damaged drape.
Then slowly and gently weave the drape of love back together again.

Don't think of a reward or about other people's criticism.
Focus only on reweaving the torn drape.

Love is like a lamp that emits a cool fire.
It brightens up the cottage of the poor man.

Always guard this love, for it is exceptionally unique.
Do not ever ask for a reward.

Love is like a fruit descended from the heavens, It is sweeter than sweet.
It only grows by spreading love and by showing patience.

June 22, 2015

پیار ایک جذبہ ہے راحت کا دل و جان کے ساتھ

یہ تو دل میں یونہی بستا ہے صبح شام کے ساتھ

تم اگر اسکو اپنے دل میں بسا لو گے تو

شام ہو جائے گی سفر کی بڑے آرام کے ساتھ

وہ جو اسکو یوں مسلتے ہیں اپنے پیروں میں

بھول جاتے ہیں کہ رب رہتا ہے دل ویران کے ساتھ۔

شگفتہ قریشی
3/11/2011

(6) Pyâr kâ jazbâ

Pyâr aik jazbâ hai râhet kâ dil-o-jân kay sâath.

Ye tû dïl meiñ yônhï bestâ hai subh-ô-shâm kay sâath.

Tum agar es kô apnay dïl meiñ bessâ lo-gye tü.

Shâm ho jaye gï safar kï beray âarâam kay sâath.

Vo jo es ko yoñ massalte heiñ ap-ne pairoñ meiñ.

Bhool jatay haiñ kay rûb rehtâ ha dil-e-vêerân kay sâath.

March 11, 2011

(6) The emotion of love

Love is an emotion of alleviation, with all your heart
and soul,
It resides in the heart, from dawn to dusk.

If you let it reside in your heart,
The Journey of your life will be pleasant.
The ones who disrespect it,
Forget that God lives in their gloomy hearts.

Shagufta Qureshi
March 11, 2011

کاش ہوتے جو الفاظ تو بیاں کر دیتی
میری حسرت کی ہوتی جو زباں ،تو بیاں کر دیتی

کاش لکھ پاتی میں بھی تیری طرح فیض
کاش رکھ پاتی وہ انداز بیاں ، تو بیاں کر دیتی

کیسے سمجھوں گی میں بلھے کی زباں
کاش لکھ پاتی قرآن ،تو بیاں کر دیتی

یہ تو وہ لوگ ہیں جو امر ہوا کرتے ہیں
یہ تو بنتے ہیں مصور کی زباں

جان پاتی وہ زباں میں
تو بیاں کر دیتی

میری معراج تو اُس راہ پہ کھڑے رہنا ہے
ساتھ اُن کے جو میں چل پاتی تو بیاں کر دیتی

وہ جو کہتے کہ لکھو اِن شاعروں پہ
کاش لکھ پاتی وہ زباں میں تو بیاں کر دیتی

شگفتہ قریشی
7/15/2014

(7) Shâair

Kâash hotae Jo alfâz tu bayâñ kar daytï
Marï hasrât kï gur hotï jo zabâñ tu bayâñ kar daytï

Kâash likh patï meiñ bhï terï tarhâ Faiz
Kâash rakh patï vo undâz-e-bayâñ tu bayâñ kar daytï

Kaise samjhôñ gï meiñ Bulleh kï zabâñ
Kâash likh pâtï meiñ Qurañ tu bayâñ kar daytï

Ye tu vo log haiñ Jo umar huwâ kertre haiñ
Ye tu bante haiñ musa-vïr kï zabâñ

Jân patï vo zabâñ meiñ
tu bayâñ kar daytï

Merï mêerâj tu us rah pe khare rehnâ hai
Sâath un-kay Jo meiñ chal patï tu bayâñ kar daytï

Vo Jo kehtay heiñ ke likhô in shayrôñ pe
Kâash likh patï vo zabâñ meiñ tu bayâñ ker daytï.

(7) The Path of poets

If only I could find the right words.
If only my wishes could speak with a tongue,
everyone could understand.

I wish I could write like you, Faiz.
If only I had that kind of expression, I could recite
poems of great meaning.

I wish my writings to be as clear as influential as
Bullah's poetry.
If only I know how to write the Quran, I would be able
to teach beautiful lessons.

Writers like Faiz and Bullah are immortal in their
poetry.
These writers are the voices of painters, painting
the truth.

I am not a writer yet; I merely stand on the path that
they walk along.
Once I learn how to walk, I will be able to tell
compelling stories.

If only those poets could teach me the right words
to say.
The perfect language to translate the truth to all
of my readers, and to allow me to walk alongside
legendary writers.

7/15/2014

کاش مسیحائی میری میری ذات میں شامل ہو جائے
کاش میرے لمس میں شفاء کا بھی اثر ہو جائے

کاش سی پاؤں میں تیرے سارے زخم
کاش بن جاؤں تیرے زخموں کی مرہم

تیری آنکھوں سے ٹپکتی ہوئی رم جھم کو کاش
اپنی مٹی دل میں، میں جذب کر پاؤں

آنکھ تیری جب کبھی بھر آتی ہے
دل تڑپتا ہے میرا جان پہ بن آتی ہے

کر سکی اور نہ کچھ بھی جو، تیری خاطر اے دوست
تیرے سنگ دو گھڑی آنسو تو بہاء سکتی ہوں

تیرے ٹوٹے ہوے خوابوں کو جو بنا نہ پائی
تیرے ٹوٹے ہوے دل کو تو اُٹھا سکتی ہوں

میں تیری شریکِ غم نہ بن پائی تو کیا
میں تیری ہم نوا بھی تو بن سکتی ہوں

کاش مسیحائی میری ذات میں شامل ہو جائے
کاش میرے لمس میں شفاء کا بھی اثر ہو جائے

شگفتہ قریشی

(8) Kâash

Kâash masïhâaï merï zâat meiñ shamïl ho jaye
Kâash mare lâms meiñ shïfâ kâ bhï aser ho jaye

Kâash sï pâoñ meiñ tare sârey zakhüm
Kâash bün jâoñ tare zakhmöñ kï mar-hüm

Tarï âankhoñ se tapktï hwï rim-jhïm ko kâash
Apnï mittï-e-dïl meiñ, maiñ jazab ker pâoñ

Âankh tarï jab kabhï bhür âatï hai
Dïl terap-tâ hai merâ, jân pe bün âatï hai

Ker sakï aur nâ kuch bhï jo, tarï khâtïr ae dost
Tare sang du gharï aansö tü bahâ saktï hoñ

Tare totey howay khoâböñ ko jo banâ nâ pâï
Tare totey howay dïl ko tü uthâ saktï hoñ

Meiñ tarï shrêek-e-ghum nâ bün pâï tü keyâ
Meiñ tarï hum-nawâ bhï tü buñ saktï hoñ

Kâash masïhâaï marï zâat meiñ shamïl ho jaye
Kâash mare lâms meiñ shïfâ kâ bhï aser ho jaye

(8) I Wish

I wish healing becomes a part of me.
I wish my touch had the ability to cure.

I wish to take care of your wounds,
I wish to be the medicine to heal you.

The raindrops falling from your eyes,
I wish I could absorb them in my heart.

Whenever your eye waters,
I lose my serenity and cannot settle myself.

If I couldn't do anything else for you, my dear friend.
At least I could share some tears with you.

If I couldn't help you save your shattered dreams,
I can comfort your broken heart.

If I couldn't be someone who shares your sorrows,
I can be your compassionate partner.

I wish healing becomes a part of me.
I wish my touch had the ability to cure.

Shagufta Qureshi.
March 9, 2016

ایک حسن دا دیوا بلدا اندروں
ایک متھے نُور چھلکدا اندروں

جنی مرضی کتاباں چا لے صاحب
اودھا سچا قول اتردا اندروں

کیوں باہر نوں چمکاوندے او
نت نئیں پوشاکاں پاندے او

اُس رب نوں راضی رکھنا اے تے
فیر دلاں نوں کیوں ڈھاندے ہو

جہڑا سبق نہ لبھے عالماں توں
اک رت جاگا سمجھا دیوے

جس اصل نوں لبھ دی رہی دُنیا
اوہ اکو سوچ بتلا دیوے

رب سوہنا اودھا ناں سوہنا
رب توں مل کے ہر جاں سوہنی

رب نوں پان لئی کیوں فیر
سوہنی نوں پھائے لاندے او

کدی جا ویکھو چھب اپنی وی
کی دُنیا نوں سمجھاندے او

جہڑا بیٹھا اے دل وچ چور بن کے
اوسے نفس توں مار کھاندے او

شگفتہ قریشی
11/17/2016

9) Ûndar

Aïk hüssan dâ dêwâ bûldâ ündroñ
Aïk mathey nôor jhlak-dâ ündroñ

Jïnï marzï kitâbâñ châ le sâheb
Ôdhâ sachâ qôl üter-dâ ündroñ

Kïyoñ bâher nü chamkân-de yö
Nït-naï pôshâ-kâñ pân-de yö

Öss rüb nü râzï rakhnâ ae te
Fïr dillâñ nü kïyoñ dhân-de hô

Jehrâ sabak nâ labhey âalmâñ tôñ
Aïk râat-jagâ Sam-jhâ de-way

Jïs assal nû labh-dï rahï dunïyâ
Ôo aiko sôoch betlâ de-way

Rûb sohnâ ôodhâ nâañ sohnâ
Rûb tôñ mïl ke her jâñ sôhnï

Rûb nôoñ pâan laï fer kïyoñ
Sôhnï nû phâ-ay lâan-de yö

Kadï jâ wakhôo chaûb apnï vï
Kï dunïyâ nû sam-jhânde yö

Jehrâ bethâa ae dïl wïch chôor bûn-ke
Ôssay nafas tôñ mâar khân-de yö

(9) Inner Beauty

A light illuminates from deep within you,
The divine light glows upon your forehead.

Regardless of all the knowledge, you acquire into
your mind,
His divine message comes only from within.

Why are you always polishing your outer-self?
By constantly changing into the newest trends.

If you wish to keep the Divine Being pleased,
Why do you insist upon breaking hearts?

The lessons that cannot be taught by the best
intellects.
Can be learned in a single night of meditation.

The reality that the world yearns for,
Can be found in a single nights' concentration.

The name of God is pure and absolute.
As is the person who follows him.

If you wish to be closer to God,
Why do you then enslave the women?

Look at your reflection,
Before you preach your beliefs to others.

Like a thief, the demon hiding in your own heart,
Is defeating you.

November 17, 2016

کھو کے ہستی کو، تُو اپنا وجود پیدا کر
بانٹ کے پیار پھر اُس بزم میں چراغاں کر دے

بن کے راہِ وفا میں پیار کی قندیل
رازِ اُلفت کو تُو دُنیا میں نمایاں کر دے

رازِ فتنہ سے اُٹھا دے پردہ
اب کسی روز کوئی ایسا تماشہ کر دے

صاحبِ عشق کو پڑھا عشق کا قول
قلبِ مرمر پہ یہ راز افشاں کر دے

اپنے آشکوں سے بجھا دِل کے اَنگار
اپنے تعلق کا کچھ ایسا تُو مقولہ کر دے

اہلِ محفل کے دِل کی کلی شگفتہ کر
بزمِ محفل میں کوئی ایسا کر شمہ کر دے۔

شگفتہ قریشی
6/11/18

(10) Râz-e-ulfat

Kho ke hasti Ko tu apna wajood paidâ ker
Bant ke pyâr tu phïr ussï bezam meiñ chiraagañ
ker de

Ban ke rah-e-wafâ meiñ pyar ki qandeel
Râz-e-ulfat ko tu duniyâ meiñ numâyañ ker de

Râz-e-fïtna se utha de perdâ
Ab kisï roz koi essâ tamashâ ker de

Sâheb-e-ïshq ko perhâ ïshq kâ qôl
Kulab-e-mar mar pe ye râz afshañ ker de

Apne ashkoñ se bujhâ dïl ke angâr
Apney tâaluq kâ kuch essâ tu makolâ ker de

Ahel-e-mehfil ke dïl ki kallï Shaguftâ ker
Bazm-e-mehfïl meiñ koï essâ karishmâ ker de!

(10) The Secret of Love

By losing your ego, you create your better self.
Spread your love, illuminate the community.

Be the candlelight in the path of faith,
Also, expose the secret of love to the world.

Expose the devil in disguise.
Perform such a unique spectacle some day.

Teach what love means to a paramour.
Unveil the secret of the stone-hearted man.

Douse the fire in your heart with your tears.
By doing so, you make your affinity phenomenal.

Bring happiness to the hearts of those
accompanying you.
Perform this magic to the flock.

June 6, 2018

(11) عُمر

پانی کے جھرنے کی مانند
بہتی چلی جاتی ھے عُمر

زندگی کے راستوں پہ
جابجا جاتی ھے عُمر

تیز چلنا چلتے رھنا
ھی تو اسکی ریت ھے

راستوں میں کیا مناظر
دکھا جاتی ھے عُمر

راستے اِسکے کبھی
کچھ ایک سے رھتے نہیں

ھمسفر بھی راہ میں
اپنے بدل جاتی ھے عُمر

بچپن کی چوکھٹ سے لیکر
آخری قیام تک

پھر دوبارہ اُس گلی
واپس نہیں آتی ھے عُمر

ریت کی مانند بند
اِن مُٹھیوں کی گرفت سے

جتنا بھی پکڑو اِسے
پھر بھی پھسل جاتی ھے عُمر

شگفتہ قریشی

9 دسمبر، 2006

Pânï ke jharne kï mânïnd
behtï chalï jâtï hai umer

Zindagï ke râastôñ pe
Jâ-bjâ jâtï hai umer

Taz chalnâ chalte rehnâ
Hï tu es kï rêet hai

Rastôñ meiñ Kyâ menâzir
dikhâ jâtï hai umer

Râstey es kay kabhï
Kuch aik say rehte nahï

Humsafar bhï râh meiñ
Apne badal jâtï hai umer

Bachpan kï chokhat se lay ker
Aakhrï qayâm tak

Phïr dobârâ us gallï
Wapes nahï âatï hai umer

Rait kï mânind
Bûnd ïn muthïyôñ kï giraft se

Jitnâ bhï pakrô issay
Phïr bhï phisal jatï hai umer.

(11) Age

Like a sprinkle of water, life keeps flowing.

Age passes through the many chapters of life.

Move fast and keep going is, in fact, life's virtue.

As life passes, it tells incredible stories.
It keeps changes its paths.

Through its journey, age changes and brings new companions.
From the infantile age until the last resting place.

Life never passes through the same path again.

Like the sand slipping through your fist,
You can keep trying, but age will always slip through.

December 9, 2006

چلو کریں آج ایک ایسا وعدہ
کبھی کہیں زندگی سے تھک کر
مسافتوں کی ڈگر سے ہٹ کر
کبھی اگر نفرتوں میں پڑ کر
جو قربتوں میں دراڑ آئے
نہ چھوڑیں گے ساتھ ایسا وعدہ

لڑائی جھگڑے وہ طعنے شکوے
وہ دل آزاری وہ کینہ پرور
کسی کو کچھ نہ ملے گا اس سے
نہ دنیا داری نہ آخرت ہی
چلو پھر ان کو بھلا کے ہم بھی
نبھا لیں یہ ساتھ ایسا وعدہ

کبھی تو سوچو کہ ساتھ کیا ہے
یہ زندگی کا ملاپ کیا ہے
زمانے بھر کی یہ داستانیں
صرف اسی پہ سمائی کیوں ہیں
وہ کون ہے جو دلوں کو باندھے
محبتوں کی بساط کیا ہے

یہ ہے وہ چشمہ کہ جس سے پھوٹے
محبتوں کے ہزار جھرنے
یہ ہے وہ نغمہ کہ جس کی دُھن پر
یہ زندگی بھی بےمست ناچے
یہ ہے وہ وعدہ جو اس کو توڑے
خدا بھی بندے سے روٹھ جائے

تو پھر وہ کیا ہے جو اس بشر کو
محبتوں سے پَرے کئے ہے
سنوُ تو ہم پھر بُھلا کے سب کچھ
چلو کریں آج ایک ایسا وعدہ
کہ زندگی کی مُسافتوں میں
نہ چھوڑیں گے ساتھ ایسا وعدہ

شگفتہ قریشی
فروری، 2013 14

(12) Aik essâ wadâ

Chalo karaiñ âaj aik essâ vâadâ
Kabhï kahïñ zindagï se thak kar
Musâfatôñ kï dagar se hât kar
Kabhï agar nafratôñ meiñ par ker
Jo qôrbatôñ meiñ darâr âye
Nâ chôraiñ ge sâath essâ vâadâ

Laraï jhagray vô tâaney shïk-way
Vô dïl âzârï vô kêenâ parwar
Kisï kô kuch nâ mïle-ga es-sey
Nâ dunyâ dâarï nâ âkhrat hï
Chalô phïr ïn-kô bhulâ ke hum bhï
Nabhâ len ye sâath essâ wâadâ

Kabhï tu sôchô ke sâath kyâ hai
Ye zindagï kâ milâp kyâ hai
Zamâne bhar kï yeh dâstâneiñ
Seraf essï pe samâï kyoñ heiñ
Vo kôn hai Jô dïlôñ kô bân-dhay
Mohabbatôñ kï bisâat Kyâ hai

Ye he vo chashmâ ke jïs se phôtay
Mohabbatôñ ke hazâr jharney
Ye he vo nagmâ ke jïs kï dhun par
Yeh zindagï bhï be-mustt nâachey
Ye he vo wadâ Jo es ko tôray
Khudâ bhï banday se rooth jaye

Tu phïr woh Kiyâ hai Jo es busher ko
Mohabbatoñ se pare kêye hai
Sunô tu hum phïr bhulâ ke sab kuch
Chalo Karaiñ âaj aik essâ wâadâ
Ke zindagï kï musafatoñ meiñ
Nâ choraiñ gay sâath essâ wâadâ.

(12) A PROMISE

Let's make a promise.
When the long paths of life wear you down, hatred can tear you apart.
Let's make a promise never to be apart.

Fighting, complaining, throwing blame, and heartbreaking arguments will not give you anything, neither in this life nor the next.
Let's forget about all of that and make a promise and hold onto each other.

Think about what companionship means?
What is the importance of relationships in life?
Why do we have to hold onto each other?
Why are all of the most popular stories about love?
What is the force that connects all of our hearts?
What is this game of love?

It is like a river that divides into a thousand springs of love.
Love is that song on that life dances in devotion.
It's that promise that when broken, makes even God unhappy.

But what is that force that keeps people from love?
Let's forget about all of that hatred and let's spread the love.
Let's promise to always hold onto each other throughout the journey of life.

February 14, 2013

کوئی تو ہے جو نئی اُمنگیں جگا رہا ہے
وہ ایک آہٹ جو چپکے سے یہ بتا رہی ہے
وہ سیدھی راہ ہے

جگائے کس نے یہ احساس سارے؟
وہ حسرت وہ نفرت عقیدت محبت
یہ سب کس نے دی ہیں؟
بہت بار سوچا بہت بار کھوجا

ضمیر کا پودا ہے کس نے بویا؟
جو حق و باطل کی پہچان کرا دے
جو الہام ہم کو بھٹکنے نہ دیں
وہ کس نے ڈالے ہیں ان دلوں میں؟

ہمارے دل میں کہیں ایک چھوٹا سا
نُور کا قطرہ جو جم سا گیا ہے
کبھی اچانک سے ٹِمٹِما کے
ہمیں وہ منزل کی سِمت بتا دے

وہ انجان طاقت
جو انسان کو ہرگام گھیرے ہوے ہے
وہ کون سی ہے؟
بہت بار سوچا بہت بار کھوجا

مگر میرے دل سے یہ آواز آئی
یہ تو بارہا ہے
یہ عزت یہ شہرت یہ ذلت
یہ سب اُس نے دی ہیں جو رب العلیٰ ہے

ہر احساس جو تم کو رستہ دکھائے
عبادت کرائے اُمیدیں جگائے
ہر الہام جو تم کو گناہ سے بچائے
وہ سب اُس نے دی ہیں جو رب العلیٰ ہے

جب پہچان لو تم اپنی خودی کو
تو جان لو گے رب کی ذات کو بھی
کہ رکھ دی ہیں اپنے ہی بندے کہ دل میں
نشانیاں رب نے پہچاننے کی!

شگفتہ قریشی

(13) Pehchân

Koï Tu hai Jo
naï umangaiñ jagâ rahâ hai
Vo aik âhet Jo chupkay say
Ye batâ rahï hai vo sêedhï râh hai

jegâye Kïs nay Ye ehsâs sârey?
Vo hussrât vo nafrât akêedat Mohabbat
Ye sub kïs dï haiñ?
Bohat bâr sochâ bohat bâr khojâ

Zamêer kâ podâ hai Kïs ne boyâ?
Jo haq-o-bâtïl kï pehchân karâ day
Jo alhâam humko bahtakney nâ deñ
vo kïs ne dâale haiñ in diloñ meiñ?

Hamâre dïl meiñ kahïñ aik chotâ sâ
Noor kâ katrâ Jo jum sâ gayâ hai
Kabhï achânak se timtimâ kay
Hume Vo manzïl kï simet batâ day

Vo unjân tâqat Jo insân ko
Her gâm ghairae huye hai
Vo kon sï hai
Bohat bâr sochâ bohat bâr khojâ

Magar mare dïl se Ye âwaz âaï
Ye Tu bâr-hâ hai
Ye izzat Ye shohrat Ye zillut
Ye sab us ne dï hai Jo rub-ul-allâ hai

Her ehsâs tum Ko jo rastâ dakhâye ibaadat karaye,
umeedaiñ jagâye
Her Ilhâam Jo gunah se bechaye
Vo sub us ne dï haiñ Jo rub-ul-allâ hai

jab pehchân lo tum apnï khudï ko
Tu mâan lo gy Rub kï zâat ko bhï
Kay rakh dï haiñ apney hï bandy kay dïl meiñ
Nïshâ-nïyâñ rub ne pehchân-nay ki

(13) Realization

There is a divine being who is creating your emotions.
Your conscious whispers to you about the right path.

Who created all of these emotions?
That envy, hate, that idealization, and that love.
Who created all of these emotions?
I ponder this often.

Who planted the seed of the conscious in our hearts?
That tells you right from wrong.
The impulse that prevents us from doing wrong.
Who planted that seed in our hearts?

Somewhere deep in our hearts is a droplet of bliss,
which is frozen.
That may suddenly sparkle some day and reveal to
us our destiny.

What is that unknown divine power that always
surrounds humankind?
I ponder this often...

However, my heart tells me this happens a lot.
The respect, fame, and dishonor…
These are all given by God.

Every sensation that shows you the right path that
urges you to worship, and that gives you hope.
Every revelation that keeps you away from sin, is
given by God.

When you find your inner conscious
You will find God too.
Because God has put the ability to find the truth in
the hearts of his people.

September 24, 2015

اے جادو نگری کے راجہ
مجھ کو بھی ایک جادو دے دے
کوئی جنتر منتر دے ایسا
کوئی جادو ٹونہ دے ویسا

تیری جادو نگری میں تو بس
سب کالے دھندے چلتے ہیں
کوئی دم درود میں پڑھتے ہیں
کہیں پتلے آگ میں جلتے ہیں

کوئی منتر تو ہو گا ایسا
جو دلوں کی میلں صاف کرے
جو نفرتوں میں ہوں پڑی ہوئی
سب جانوں کو آزاد کرے

جب دیکھوں تو یوں لگتا ہے
جیسے کیکر کے اُن کانٹوں میں
جیون کی پتنگ ہے پھنسی ہوئی
کچھ پھٹی ہوئی کچھ بچی ہوئی

تو سارے دھندے رکھ اپنے
بس ایک کی ڈور مجھے دے دے
جس دل کو تو پامال کرے
اُس دل کو میں بحال کروں

کچھ ایسا کر کے ساری جنگ
تیری میری ہی ہو جائے
ایک لمحے کو ہی کاش مگر
یہ دنیا جنت ہو جائے

اے جادو نگری کے راجہ
مجھ کو بھی ایک جادو دے دے
کوئی جنتر منتر دے ایسا
کوئی جادوُ ٹونہ دے ویسا

شگفتہ قریشی
12/9/2016

(14) Jâadu Nagrï

Ay jâadû nagrï ke râajâ
Mujh ko bhï aik jâadu de-day
Koï jantar muntar de essâ
Koï jâadu tônâ de wessâ

Terï jâadu nagrï meiñ tu bas
Sab kâle dhûn-de chalte haiñ
Koï dum-dârôd meiñ parte haiñ
Kahêeñ pûtlay âag meiñ jaltey haiñ

Koï mantar tu hô gâ essâ
Jô dïlôñ kï maïlaiñ sâaf karey
Jô nafratôñ meiñ parï hovï
Sab jâanô kô âazâd karey

Jab dekhôñ tû youñ lagtâ hai
Jassey kïker ke ïn kântôñ pe
Jêewan kï patang hai phasï hovï
Kuch phatï hovï, kuch bachï hovï

Tû sâaray dhûn-de rakh apne
Bas aik kï dôor mujhey de-day
Jïs dïl kô tu pâamâl karey
Us dïl kô meiñ bahâl karoñ

Kuch essâ ker ke sâarï jang
Tarï merï hï hô jâye
Aik lamhey kô hï kâash mager
Ye dunïyâ janat hô jâye

Ay jâadû nagrï ke râajâ
Mujh ko bhï aik jâadu de-day
Koï jantar muntar de essâ
Koï jâadu tônâ de wessâ.

(14) World of Magic

O. king of the world of magic,
Give me one magical power, teach me a spell, or give me a magic wand.

In your mystical world, there is black magic — sorcerers who mumble curses and burn wooden dolls.

There has to be a spell that can clean one's heart. There has to be a spell or trick that frees people from hatred.

When I look at the world, I see that it is wounded. It's full of pros and cons like puncture holes through a beautiful kite that is trapped in a Thorny bush.

You can keep all of your dark magic. Just give me the power to repair a broken heart, to give directions to a lost soul, and to give light to those that are consumed by darkness.

Can we keep the war of good and evil between us? At least for that moment, the world will become a blissful paradise.

O king of the world of magic,
Give me one magical power, teach me a spell, or give me a magic wand.

December 9, 2016

(15) دل کی مٹی

یہ دل کی مٹی عجیب شئے ہے
یہ نفرتوں اور عداوتوں کی
ملاوٹوں سے بنی ہے شائد
یہ دل کی مٹی عجیب شئے ہے

کہیں محبت کی ہے ملاوٹ
کہیں حسد کی ہے چھاپ اس پر
کہیں عبادت کی دلدلوں میں
پھنسی ہوئی ہے زمین اس کی

کہیں یہ خود پسندی سے گوندھی ہے
کہیں نشہ اپنے حسن کا ہے
کہیں حکومت وہ چاہتی ہے
کہیں ہوس اس کی تاثیر میں ہے

کہیں ہے دولت کی چاہ اس کو
کہیں فراغت سے راہ اس کو
کہیں ہے کینہ بغض اور غیبت
سمجھے نہ یہ کام کی لگی ہے
یہ دل کی مٹی عجیب شئے ہے

کوئی بھی احساس گر ہو غالب
تو دل کرے وہ ، جو وہ کرائے
محبتوں کا اسیر بندہ
محبتوں کو خدا بنائے

کوئی جو ہو حسد کا مارا
وہ حاسدوں کی تقدیر پائے
جو چاہتا ہو بس حکمرانی
اُسے رعایا ہی نظر آئے

جو غیبتوں میں پھنسا ہوا ہو
وہ سب کو بتلائے اک کہانی
جو ہو کوئی اپنی انا کا محصور
وہ بس خدائی کا زوم پائے

عبادتوں میں پھنسے ہووں کو
ستائشوں میں پڑے ہووں کو
تمام دنیا ہی کھوٹی لگی ہے
یہ کیسی دلدل میں جا پھنسی ہے

یہ دل کی مٹی عجیب شئے ہے
کسی بھی مٹی سے گو بنے دل
کوئی بھی تاثیر ہو اس میں شامل
مجھے تو اس میں کمی ملی ہے

کمی ہے بس یکسانیت کی
کمی ہے اس میں انسانیت کی
وہ سب سے بہتر تو دیکھے خود کو
مگر سبھی کو حقیر جانے

یہ نفرتوں اور عداوتوں کی
ملاوٹوں سے بنی ہے شاید
مجھے نہ یہ کام کی لگی ہے
یہ دل کی مٹی عجیب شئے ہے!!!!

شگفتہ قریشی
7/01/2017

(15) Dïl kï mattï

Ye dïl kilï mattilï ajêeb shay hai
Ye naffertoñ aur adâwatoñ kï
Milâvtôñ se banï hai shayad
Ye dïl kï mattï ajeeb shay hai

Kahiñ mohabbat ki hai milâwat
Kahiñ hasad kï hai châp es per
Kahiñ ibaadat kï daldaloñ meiñ
Phansï huï hai zamin es kï

Kahiñ ye khud pasandï se gondhï hai
Kahiñ nashâ apne hussan kâ hai
Kahiñ hukumat vo chahtï hai
Kahiñ hiwas es ki tasseer meiñ hai

Kahiñ hai dolat ki châh es ko
Kahiñ faraghat se râh es ko
Kahiñ hai keenâ, bughz aur gheebat
Mujhe nâ ye kâam kï lagï hai

Ye dïl kï mattï ajeeb shay hai

Koi bhi ehsaas gar ho ghalib
Tu dil kare vo, jo vo karâye
Mohabbatoñ kâ assiêr bandâ
Mohabbatoñ ko khudâ banaye

Koi jo ho hasad ka marâ
Vo haasidoñ kï taqdeer paye
Jo chatâ ho bas hukmranï
ussey reaayâ hï nazar aaye

Jo ghêebtoñ meiñ phansâ hua ho
Vo sab ko batlaye aik kahanï
Jo ho koi apnï anâa kâ mehsôr
Vo bas khudaï kâ zoam paye

Ibadatoñ meiñ phansey huvoñ ko
Setâa-e-shoñ meiñ pare howoñ ko
Tamâm duniâ hï khotï lagï hai
Ye kessï daldal meiñ jâ phansï hai

Ye dïl kï mattï ajêeb shay hai
Kisï bhï mattï se goh bane dïl
Koï bhï tâsêer ho es meiñ shamïl
Mujhe tu es meiñ kamï milï hai

Kamï hai bas yaksânïyet kï
Kamï hai es meiñ insânïyet kï
Vo sab se behtar tu dekhay khud ko
Mager sabhï ko haqêer jâne

Ye naffroñ aur adâwatoñ kï
Milâvtoñ se banï hai shayad
Mujhe nâ ye kâam kï lagï hai
Ye dïl kï mattï ajêeb shay hai!

(15) Heart's soil

The soil of the heart is a strange thing.
I think it's made by the fusion of hatred and
vengeance.
The soil of the heart is a strange thing.

Sometimes it blends with love,
Sometimes it gives the impression of jealousy.
However, sometimes it's stuck in the quagmire of
worship.

Sometimes it is narcissistic,
Sometimes it gets high on its beauty.
Sometimes it wants power,
Sometimes lust can be found within its soil.

Sometimes it wants wealth,
Sometimes it just wants to be lazy.
Sometimes it's made out of grudges, gossip, and
malice.
In any shape or form it takes, I am not too fond of it.

No matter which of the senses are dominant,
Your heart will do whatever that sense wants it to do.
The person who is infatuated with love will worship
love.

Whoever is infused with jealousy will receive the fate
of a jealous person.
The one who wants power will see people as his
slaves.

Those who gossip will tell people a slandered story.
The person who is controlled by his narcissism turns
himself into a demon.

Those who were caught with excess worship, see the world as a mutilated coin.
What kind of quagmire do they find themselves in?

The soil of the heart is a strange thing.
No matter what kind of soil it is infused with, no matter what kind of ramifications it has. I find it inadequate.

I find that the soil of the heart has inadequate equality and deficient of humanity.
It finds itself on top and sees everyone else beneath it.

I think the heart's soil made by the fusion of hatred and vengeance.
In any shape or form it takes, I am not too fond of it.
The soil of the heart is a strange thing.

July 7, 2017

یہ چاند اُفق پر صدیوں سے
آتا ہے اور وہ دیکھتا ہے
انسانوں کی جو بستی ہے
اس میں ہنسہ کو دیکھتا ہے

یہ کون ہیں اِس دُنیا والے؟
یہ کِس مٹی سے پیدا ہوے؟
یہ اپنی ہی قوم کو روندتے ہیں
اپنی ہی نسل کھانے والے

کبھی سُنا تھا میں نے
سانپ جو تھا اپنے بچے کھا جاتا تھا
اس دنیا کا انسان بھی تو
اپنی ہی نسل کھا جاتا ہے

وہ دیکھتے ہیں جو دکھتا ہے
وہ دل کے اندر جھانکتے نہیں
کب رنگ اور کیڑوں سے بھی کوئی
کیا جان سکا ہے نیت کو؟

یہ چاند افق پر صدیوں سے
آتا ہے اور وہ دیکھتا ہے

دل کہتا ہے یہ دنیا تو
اس غرض بنائی تھی رب نے
جہاں رنگ برنگے لوگوں کو
حاصل ہو بس انساں ہونا

جہاں خلق خدا ہو نیک طبع
جہاں جان و مال اور عزت سے
بڑھ کر نہ ہو
کوئی جزا

اِس چاند نے تو دیکھا ہو گا
آدم سے مُحمّد تک سب کچھ
کہاں پیار ہوا اِنسانوں میں
کہاں جان کے دشمن بن گے سب

اب کیسے یہ رنجش ہو گی دور؟
ہوگا کیسے اِنساں کا مِلن؟

اے کاش کہ وہ موسم آئے
جب چاند زمیں پہ مسکائے
جہاں پیار اور امن کی گود ہیں
اِنسان اشرف المخلوقات کہلاے

یہ چاند اُفق پر صدیوں سے
آتا ہے اور وہ دیکھتا ہے
یہ چاند افق پہ صدیوں سے
اور کب تک یہ سب دیکھے گا؟؟؟

شگفتہ قریشی
12/10/2015

(16) Chând kï Nagrï

Ye chând ôofaq per sadïyôñ se
Âatâ hai aur vô dekhtâ hai.
Insânô kï jô bastï hai
Es meiñ hinsâ ko dekhtâ hai.

Ye kôn hain es dunïyâ wale?
Ye kïs mattï se pedâ howay?
Ye apnï hï qôm kô rond-te haiñ?
Apnï hï nessal khâne wale?

Kabhï sunâ thâ meiñ ne
Sâanp jô thâ apne bachay khâ
jatâ thâ.
Es dunïyâ kâ insâan bhï tu
Apnï hï nessal khâ jatâ hai.

Vo dekh-te haiñ jo dikh-tâ hai
Vo dïl kay undar jhânk-te nahï.
Kab rung aur kaprôñ se bhï koï
Kyâ jân sakâ hai nêeyât ko?

Ye chând ôofaq per sadïyôñ se
Âatâ hai aur vô dekhtâ hai.

Dïl kehtâ hai ye dunïyâ tu
Es gharz banâï thï rûb ne.
Jâhâñ rung-b-rungay lôogôñ ko
Hâasïl ho bas insâañ hônâ.

Jâhâñ khûlk-e-khudâ hô
Naik tâbâh .
Jâhâñ jâan, mâal aur izûet se
Burh ker nâ hô koï jazâ.

Es chând ne tu dekhâ ho-gâ
Âdam se Muhammad tuk
sab-kuch.
Kahâñ payâr hwa insâano meiñ.
Kahân jâan ke dushmân bûn gye sab .

Ab kassy ye rûnjish ho gï dôr?
Ho gâ kassy insâañ kâ millan ?

Aye kâash ke vo mousâm âaye.
Jab chând zameiñ per mouskâye.
Jâhâñ payâr aur amen kï gôad meiñ.
In-sâan ush-râful makhlô-kâat kehlâye.

Ye chând ôofaq per sadïyôñ se
Âatâ hai aur vô dekhtâ hai.
Ye chând ôofaq per sadïyôñ se
Aur kab tak ye-sab dekhey gâ?

(16) Moon on world

For centuries the moon watched the earth from above and thought.
It sees the human cities, and it sees the chaos.

Who are these people and what ethics do they have?
Who fights their communities and who feed on their generation when hungry.

I have heard once that snakes eat their children.
Humans are also destroying their generation.

They see cosmetic flaws, and they don't look into hearts.
Can anyone find their good nature just by looking at the color of their skin and the clothing they wear?

My heart says that God made this world because people of different color and different faith can live in harmony.

Where people respect each other and where life is precious.

This moon must have seen the timeline from Adam to Muhammad.
When humans loved each other to when they become rivals.

Now, how will this misunderstanding be resolved?
And how will humans become friends again?

I wish the atmosphere would change.
So that the moon looks down from above and smiles,
At a world where humans live in peace and love
As the most divine creations of God.

For centuries the moon watched the earth from above and thought.
How long does it have to see all this?

December 10, 2015

کس ناگ راج کے باسی ہم
وہ جنگل راج تو بہتر تھا

اس دنیا کا قانون مگر
جنگل کا راج تو بہتر تھا

جہاں وحشی اپنے شکار کے بعد
چپ چاپ چھاؤں میں سوتا تھا

جہاں سانپ نیولا ناگن سب
اک ریت رواج سے رہتے تھے

ہم کس دیس میں رہتے ہیں
جو ریت رواج میں بندھ نہ سکیں

جو بھر پیٹ کھا لینے کے بعد
دو گھڑی سکوں بھی کر نہ سکیں

ایسی لالچ ایسی کیا بھوک
جو جانوروں سے بھی بدتر ہو

کس ناگ راج کے باسی ہم
وہ جنگل راج تو بہتر تھا

اب کاش اُس جنگل کا قانون
میرے دیس میں بھی چھا جائے

جب سانپ نیولا ناگن سا
میرا حکمراں بھی سو جائے

تم دیکھو گے سو جانے کے بعد
کتنی جانیں بچ جائیں گیں

اس دنیا کا قانون بھی تو
جنگل کی طرح ہو جائے گا

کب وہ دن ایسا آئے گا
کب وہ دن ایسا آئے گا

شگفتہ قریشی

نومبر 16, 2014

(17) Nâg Râj

Kis nâg râj ké bâasi hum
Vo jangal râj tu behtar thâ

Es duniya ka qanoôn magar
Jangle kâ râj tu behtar thâ

Jahañ vehshï apne shikâr ke bâad
Chup châp châoñ meiñ sôotâ thâ

Jahâñ sânp névola nagan sūb
Aik rēet riwâj meiñ rehte thae

Hum kïs dais meiñ rehtè haiñ
Jo reet riwâj meiñ buñdh na sakaiñ

Jo bhûr pait khâ lene ke bâad
Dû gharï sakooñ bhi kar na sakaiñ

Àssï lâ-lûch àssï keya bhook
Jo jânwarôñ se bhï bad-tur hô

Kis nâg râj ké bâasi hum
Vo jangal râj tu behtar thâ

Ab kâash us jangâl kâ qanoon
Merey dais maiñ bhï châ jayè

Jab sânp, névola, nâgan sâ
Merâ hukmerâñ bhï so jajé

Tum dekho gay so jâné ke bâad
Kitnï jânaiñ buch jaye gï

Es duniyâ kâ qânoon bhï tu
Jangle kï terhâ ho jayé gâ

Kab vo dïn essâ aye ga?
Kab vo din essâ aye ga?

(17) The Dark Realm

What kind of dark realm do we live in?
The Laws of the jungle are better than the laws of
the land.

Our world is full of lawlessness and cruelty.
The jungle is full of order and serenity.

Where vicious animals, after hunting their prey,
quietly sleep under the shadow of a tree.
Where snakes, ferrets, pythons all live by their customs.

What kind of world are we living in? Where there are
no similar customs.
Where they keep on hunting others but are not able
to rest peacefully.

Such greed, such appetite makes us worse than animals.

What dark realm are we living in?
The laws of the animals are better.

I pray that the law of the jungle becomes the law of
the land.
Where the ruler of land learns humility from wild animals.

You will see by doing so; many lives will be saved.
I wish the laws of the land would parallel the law of
the jungle.

When would such day arrive?

Shagufta Qureshi
November 16, 2014

تیرے میرے پیار کے درمیاں
یہ جو آنسوں کی خلیج ہے

یہ تو چند قدم کے تھے فاصلے
اب میلوں میں کیوں محیط ہیں؟

کیوں ہیں گہرے نیلے سمندر سے؟
کیوں ہیں ساکت ان خالاؤں سے؟

اسے کیسے کریں گے پار ہم؟
میری نیہ بیچ منجدھار ہے

کبھی سوچنا کہ یہی تھی کیا؟
جو تھی راہ ہمارے پیار کی

کیا اسی کی خاطر ملے تھے ہم؟
کہ کریں گے زخمی اُسی کو ہم؟

مجھے اپنی انا عزیز تھی
تجھے اپنی ضد سے ہی پیار ہے

کئی سال اس میں غرق ہوئے
کئی لمحوں کا اب ملال ہے

ابھی اور کتنا تڑپنا ہے؟
ابھی اور کب یہ وصال ہے؟

یہ خلیج تو ہے نگل گئ
تیرے میرے گھر کے قرار کو

کہ اسی کی گود میں دفن ہیں
وہ جو کونپلیں کبھی پھوٹی تھیں

شگفتہ قریشی

3/27/2016

(18) Khalêej

Tare mare payâr ke darmiyâñ
Ye jo âansôvoñ kï khalêej hai

Ye tu chund kadam ke thay fâsle
Ab mêlôñ meiñ keyoñ mohêt haiñ?

Kïyoñ haiñ gehray nêlay sumondar se ?
Kïyoñ haiñ sâaket in khlâoñ se?

Essy kay-sy karaiñ gy par hum?
Merï nïyâ beach mujh-dâr hai.

Kabhï sochnâ ke yehï thï keyâ ?
Jo thï râah hamârey payâr kï?

Keyâ issï kï khâtïr mïle thay hum?
Ke karaiñ gy zakhmï issï ko hum?

Mujhey apnï anâa aziz thï.
Tujhay apnï zïd se hï payâr hai.

Kaï sâal es meiñ ghrak howay.
Kaï lamhôñ kâ ab melâal hai.

Abhï aur kïtnâ tarap-nâ hai?
Abhi aur kab ye wasâal hai?

Ye khalêej tu hai nïgal gaï
Tare mare ghar ke kerâar ko.

Ke issï kï goad meiñ dufun haiñ.
Vô jo komplaiñ kabhï phôotï thï.

(18) The gulf

In between our love,
there's a gulf of tears.

The distance between us was only a few steps,
Why now is it miles apart?

Why is it deep, like the ocean?
Why is it silent, like in space?

How can we cross this gulf between us?
I am right in the middle of the maelstrom.

Sometimes I wonder,
If that's the way, we want our love to be?

Did we meet for this?
To hurt our love?

I liked my ego,
You loved your stubbornness.

We lost many years like this.
With the regrets of many moments.

How long do we have to feel this agony?
How long before we can meet again?

That gulf of tears had engulfed,
A century of our home.

The sprouts born in this relationship,
Are buried deep in the gulf.

March 27, 2016

کبھی سوچا میرے جاناں کہ گر ہم نہ ملے ہوتے
کبھی سوچا کہ راہوں میں تیری ہم نہ رہے ہوتے

تمہاری یاد کو دل سے لگا کے جی تو لیتے ہم
مگر یہ جان لو جاناں کوئی جینا نہیں ہوتا

جو رہتے ہم اگر انجان دلبر ہم سفر کے ساتھ
میری چاہ و محبت میں کوئی جذبہ نہیں ہوتا

جو مِلتا زندگی سے اُس پہ شائد صبر کر لیتے
لیکن یادوں کی نگری میں بھٹک کر رو رہے ہوتے

کبھی سوچا میرے جاناں کہ گر ہم نہ ملے ہوتے
کبھی سوچا کہ راہوں میں تیری ہم نہ رہے ہوتے

ہم اپنی زندگی تو جیسے تیسے کاٹ ہی لیتے
تمہاری زندگی کا حال کیا ہم سے جدا ہوتا؟

تمہاری زندگی میں بھی کسک رہ جاتی اے جاناں
تمہاری آنکھ میں بھی شبنم کا قطرہ جما ہوتا

کبھی جو ہم اگر ملتے کسی انجان محفل میں
نظر تیری بھری محفل میں کیا مجھ پر ٹھہر جاتی؟

کہیں جو راہ گزر میں گر ہمارا سامنا ہوتا
کیا ہم انجان لوگوں کی طرح ہر بات کہہ پاتے؟

یا پھر نظریں چُرا کے آپ سے یونہی چلے جاتے
سسکتے لفظوں میں یا پھر صرف آداب ہی کرتے

کبھی سوچا میرے جاناں کہ گر ہم نہ ملے ہوتے
.کبھی سوچا کہ راہوں میں تیری ہم نہ رے ہوتے

شگفتہ قریشی
نومبر 24، 2014

(19) Jâanâ

Kabhï sochâ mere Jâanâ
Ke gur hum nâ Mïley hotay
Kabhï sochâ ke rahoñ meiñ terï
Hum nâ rahe Hotay

Tumhârï yâad ko dïl se lagâ ke
Jï tu letay hum
Magur ye jâan lo Jâanâ
Koï Jêenâ nahï hotâ

Jo rehte hum agur unjan
dil-bûr Humsafar ke sâath
Marï châ-ô-mohabbat meiñ
Koï jazbâ nahï hotâ

Jo miltâ zindagï se us pe
Shâyed Sabar kar letay
Lakïn yâdôñ kï nagrï meiñ
Bhatak ke rô rahe hotay

Kabhï sochâ mere Jâanâ
Ke gur hum nâ Miley hotay
Kabhï sochâ ke rahoñ meiñ terï
Hum na rahe hotey

Ham apnï zindagï tu
jai-se tai-se Kâat hï letay
Tumharï zindagï kâ hâl
Keyâ hum se judâ hotâ?

Tumharï zindagï meiñ bhï
Kasak reh jatï aye Jâanâ
Tumharï âankh meiñ bhï
Shabnam kâ qetrâ jamâ hotâ

Kabhï Jo hum ager miltay
Kisï anjan mehfïl meiñ
Nazar terï bharï mehfïl meiñ
Kyâ mujh per taher jatï ?

Kabhï Jo rah-guzar meiñ
Gur hamara samnâ hotâ
Kya hum anjân logoñ kï terhâ
Her bâat kah pâtay?

Yâ phïr nazreñ churâ ke
Âap-se yoñhï chalay jâtey
Sisak-tay lehjay maiñ yâ phïr
Sïraf âadâb hï kretay.

Kabhï sochâ mere Jâanâ
Ke gur hum nâ Milay hotay
Kabhï sochâ ke rahon meiñ terï
Hum nâ rahe hotay.

(19) Darling

Have you ever thought, my love, what if we never met?
Have you ever thought if our paths never crossed?

I would have lived with your memories in my heart
However, life would have been meaningless

If I would have lived with an unknown affiliate,
Love and affections would have been
compassion-less.

I would have accepted whatever life would have
given to me.
However, I would always be yearning in my memories.

Have you ever thought, my love, what if we never met?
Have you ever thought if our paths never crossed?

I would have lived my life one way or the other.
Would you have had a life different than mine?

Your life would also be empty, my love.
With a tear lingering in your eye.

If by chance we met at a gathering.
Would you have kept on looking at me?

If we have ever come across each other,
Could we have spoken just like strangers?

Or would we have looked away as we passed each
other?
Or would we be able to say "hi" through quivering
lips?

Have you ever thought, my love, what if we never met?
Have you ever thought if our paths never crossed?

Shagufta Qureshi
November 24, 2014

شام کی مانند مرے شانے پہ بکھر جائے تیری زلف
اور میں موم کی صورت میں پگھلتا جاؤں

تیری خوشبو سے مہک جائے مرا سارا وجود
اور میں عشق کی وادی میں اُترتا جاؤں

ساتھ تیرے جو گزر جائے وہی وقت اپنا
باقی لمحوں کو تیری یاد میں چنتا جاؤں

جان میری تجھے کیسے کہوں میں حال اپنا
میں تو پل پل تیری چاہت میں تڑپتا جاؤں

شام کی مانند مرے شانے پہ بکھر جائے تیری زلف
اور میں موم کی صورت میں پگھلتا جاؤں

شگفتہ قریشی
18 اکتوبر 2017

(20) Teri Zûlf

Shâm ki mânind mere shâné pe bikhar jaye teri zûlf
Aur mein moam ki sorat mein pigalta jaoñ

Teri khushboo se mehak jaye mera sara wajod
Aur mein ishq ki vâadi mein utarta jaoñ

Sâth tere jo guzer jaye vohi waqat apna
Baki lamhon ko teri yaad mein chunta jaoñ

Jan meri tujhe kessey kahooñ mein hâl apna
Mein tu pal pal teri chahat mein tarapta jaoñ

Sham ki mânind mere shâné pe bikhar jaye teri zûlf
Aur mein moam ki sorat mein pigalta jaoñ!!

(20) Your hair

Like an evening, spread your hair on my shoulder,
And I will keep melting in your love.

My whole existence gets saturated with your aroma
and I keep falling in love with you, even more.

Moments spent with you are the life of me.
I spend the rest of time thinking about you.

How can I describe my devotion to you, my love?
I desire your love every single moment.

Like an evening, spread your hair on my shoulders,
And I keep melting in your love.

Shagufta Qureshi
October 18th, 2017

زندگی کے رستے میں ساتھ چلتے رہنا ہے
راستہ کٹھن بھی ہو، تو آگے بڑھتے رہنا ہے

راستوں کی مشکل سے تم ڈر نہیں جانا
مشکلیں تو آتیں ہیں ہمتیں بڑھانے کو

ہمتوں کے رہنے سے ساتھ نبھتے رہتے ہیں
ہمتوں کو رکھنا ہے ساتھ کو بچانا ہے

ہار سے کبھی بھی تم ہارنا نہ جانِ من
ہار تو سکھاتی ہے جیت کیسے پاتے ہیں

جیتنا تمھیں ہر دم کر نہ دے کہیں خود سر
خود سری سے بچنے کو ہارنا ضروری ہے

زندگی کے رستے میں ساتھ چلتے رہنا ہے
راستہ کٹھن بھی ہو آگے بڑھتے رہنا ہے

شگفتہ قریشی
اکتوبر 2017 19

(21) Zindagï

Zindagï ke râste meiñ sâath chalte rehnâ hai
Râsstâ kathân bhï ho, tü âage barh-te rehnâ hai

Râsstöñ kï mushkïl se tum dâr nahï janâ
Mushkï-leiñ tu âatï haiñ hemat-aiñ berhâ-ne ko

Hematôñ ke rehne se sâath nibh-te rehte haiñ
Hematôñ ko rakhnâ hai sâath ko bechânâ hai

Hâar se kabhï bhï tum hârnâ nâ jân-e-mün
Hâar tu sikhâtï hai jêet kasse pâte haiñ

Jêetnâ tumheiñ her-dûm ker nâ dey kaheiñ khud-sar
Khud-sarï se bachne ko hâr-nâ zarôorï hai

Zindagï ke râste meiñ sâath chalte-rehnâ hai
Rastey kathân bhï ho, tü âage barh-te rehnâ hai.

(21) Life

One must always travel onward through the path of life.
No matter how difficult it gets, keep marching forward.

Don't be afraid of the challenges in your way.
These challenges are there to strengthen you with the courage to keep moving forward.

Your Courageousness helps you to strengthen your relationships.
Holding onto that courage will preserve your relationships.

My dear, never be afraid of failure, it teaches you how to succeed.
Constant success will make you arrogant; failure is the only cure against arrogance.

Keep marching onward together with those you love, along with the path of life.
No matter how difficult it gets, always move forward.

October 19, 2017

اِئے کاش کہ اب اس دھرتی پہ
ایک اور مسیحا پیدا ہو

اِن مایوسی میں ڈوبوں کا
ایک اور وصیلہ پیدا ہو

جو کالی راتیں ختم کرئے
جو جنگ کی باتیں ختم کرئے

جو انسانوں سے پیار کرئے
کوئی ایک تو ایسا پیدا ہو

اِئے کاش کہ اب اس دھرتی پہ
ایک اور مسیحا پیدا ہو

اِس رنگ برنگی دنیا کو
جو رنگوں سے بھر دنے ایسے

جہاں مذہب ایمان کی بات نہیں
بس انسانیت کا نعرہ ہو

جہاں جان بڑی انمول ہو
سکھ چین کی بانسری بجتی ہو

اِئے کاش کہ اب اس دھرتی پہ
ایک اور مسیحا پیدا ہو

اِئے کاش کہ اب اس دھرتی پہ
کوئی ایسا مسیحا پیدا ہو

شگفتہ قریشی

4/12/2013

(22) Masêehâ

Aye kâah ke ab es dhartï pe
Aik aur masêehâ pedâ ho

In mâyosï meiñ dôbôñ kâ
Aik aur wasêelâ pedâ ho

Jo kâlï râataiñ khatûm kere
Jo jang kï bâataiñ khatûm kere

Jo ïnsâanô se pyâr kere
Koï aik tu es-sâ pédâ ho

Aye kâsh ke ab es hartï pe
Aik aur masêehâ pedâ ho

Es rang birangï duniyâ ko
Jo rangoñ se bhar de esse

Jahâñ mazhab êmâan kï bâat nahï
Bus ïnsânïyt kâ narâ ho

Jahâñ jan barï un-môl ho
Sukh chain bansurï bajtï ho

Aye kâsh ke ab-es hartï pe
Aik aur masêehâ pedâ ho.

Aye kâsh ke ab-es hartï pe
Koï aisâ masêehâ pedâ ho.

(22) Messiah

I wish for the birth of another Messiah in our world.

Some people are in despair, people who need to be shown hope.

The world needs someone to shed light on those dark and stormy nights.

The world needs one hero, to end its war.

Someone who loves people.
I wish for the birth of another Messiah.

Who can repaint our world with more vibrant colors?

a world where humanity is more important than religion or character.

Where life is precious, and peace is everywhere.

I wish for the birth of that Messiah in our world.

April 12, 2013

باندھ لو پھر سے مجھے آج اُسی سچائی سے
جیسے باندھا تھا کبھی آپ نے آشنائی سے

آج پھر تھام کے بولو میرا ہاتھ یہ تم
زندگی تم ہو، میرا ماضی بھی میرا حال بھی تم

میرے بچپن سے جوانی کی ہو پہچان بھی تم
زندگی کے ہر ایک گوشے کے راز داں بھی ہو تم

جب کبھی پیار میں اتنا سفر کر جاتے ہیں
تب تو چاہت بھی عبادت میں بدل جاتی ہے

باندھ لو پھر مجھے آج اُسی سچائی سے
جیسے باندھا تھا کبھی آپ نے آشنائی سے!!!

شگفتہ قریشی

(23) Bandhan

Bândh lô phïr se mujhe
Âj ussi sachaai sê

Jessay bañdhâ thâ kabhï
Âp ne âshnâï se

Âj phïr thâm ke bolô
Mera hâth ye tum

Zindagi tum ho
Mera mâzi bhi merâ hal bhi tum

Meray bachpan se
Jawani ki ho pehchan bhi tum

Zindagi ke har ek goshay kï
Raz-dâñ bhi ho tum

Jab kabhï pyâr meiñ
Itna safar ker jate haiñ

Tab tu chahat bhï
Ibadet me badal jati hai

Bândh lo phïr se mujhe
Âj ussï sachâi se

Jassay bandha thâ kabhï
Âp ne âshnâï se!

(23) The Bond

Hold me once again with the same pureness
Like you once did with acceptance

Repeat it today, holding my hand
That you are my life, my past and my future.

You've known me from childhood to adulthood.
You are the trusted partner who knows every moment
of my life.

Whenever your love lasts this long,
then the love relation becomes worship

Hold me once again with the same pureness
Like you once did with acceptance.

Shagufta Qureshi.

Printed and bound by PG in the USA